FUN SCIENCE

Experiments in

LIGHT AND SOUND

with Toys and Everyday Stuff

BY NATALIE ROMPELLA

raintree

a Capstone company — publishers for children

Raintree is an imprint of Capstone Global Library Limited, a company incorporated in England and Wales having its registered office at 7 Pilgrim Street, London, EC4V 6LB – Registered company number: 6695582

**www.raintree.co.uk**
myorders@raintree.co.uk

Edited by Alesha Sullivan
Designed by Kyle Grenz
Picture research by Jo Miller
Production by Kathy McColley

ISBN 978 1 474 70355 0
19 18 17 16 15
10 9 8 7 6 5 4 3 2 1

**British Library Cataloguing in Publication Data**
A full catalogue record for this book is available from the British Library.

**Acknowledgements**
Capstone Studio/Karon Dubke except: Shutterstock: Katrina Leigh, cover (rubberbands), koya979, cover (blocks), MichealJayBerlin, cover (black marker), MNI, cover (colored papers)

We would like to thank Paul Ohmann, PhD, Associate Professor of Physics at the University of St. Thomas in St. Paul, Minnesota, for his invaluable help in the preparation of this book.

Every effort has been made to contact copyright holders of material reproduced in this book. Any omissions will be rectified in subsequent printings if notice is given to the publisher.

All the internet addresses (URLs) given in this book were valid at the time of going to press. However, due to the dynamic nature of the internet, some addresses may have changed, or sites may have changed or ceased to exist since publication. While the author and publisher regret any inconvenience this may cause readers, no responsibility for any such changes can be accepted by either the author or the publisher.

Printed in China.

# CONTENTS

# TURN YOUR HOUSE INTO A SCIENCE LAB!

For some science projects you need special equipment and laboratories. But other **experiments** can be done in your own home. You can even use your toys and other everyday items!

**experiment** scientific test to find out how something works

Fireworks, thunder, glow sticks and films all involve light or sound in special ways. Have you ever wondered how sound and light work around you every day? Get ready to uncover the mysteries of sound and light as you learn about science!

**TURN TO PAGE 20 TO SEE HOW THE SCIENCE WORKS IN EACH EXPERIMENT!**

# FRIGHT NIGHT

If you step outside into the sunshine, you'll see your **shadow** on the ground. You may wonder why your shadow changes shape and length sometimes. Get together with a friend or sibling and have a night of fright while playing with shadows!

Materials:

torch

stuffed animal or action figure

paper

scissors

**shadow** dark shape made when something blocks light

## Steps:

1. **Turn off the lights and close any blinds or curtains to make the room dark.**

2. **Put the torch in front of a stuffed animal or action figure. Move the torch closer to and further away from your toy. What does its shadow look like?**

3. **Use the scissors to cut some shapes out of paper to make scary shadows, such as a wolf or ghost. Shine the light in front of the shapes. Move the torch around to see different shadows. How can you make the shadows the scariest?**

4. **Put on a show for a friend!**

# SUN POWER

On a clear, summer's day the Sun can feel really hot! If you're outside for too long, you may even get sunburnt. See for yourself how **ultraviolet light** from the Sun reaches Earth's surface.

## Materials:

scissors

2 rocks

2 pieces of coloured construction paper

sun cream

empty plastic CD case

a small, heavy toy

## Tip:

If you can't do this project outside, try attaching the coloured paper to a window facing the Sun for a couple of days. Compare the two sides of the paper.

**ultraviolet light** invisible form of light that can cause sunburn

## Steps:

1. Find a spot outside that is in direct sunlight.

2. Use scissors to cut one sheet of paper so it fits inside of the CD case. Put a small amount of sun cream on the outside of the CD case.

3. Put the CD case and the other piece of paper in the Sun. Weigh the paper down with rocks on the corners. Place the toy in the middle of the paper.

4. Allow the CD case and paper to sit in the Sun for 2 to 3 hours.

5. Remove the toy from the paper. What happened to the paper that wasn't covered by the toy?

6. Slide the piece of paper out of the CD case. What happened to the part of the paper that wasn't covered by the sun cream?

9

# REFLECTION PAINTING

Look closely at your face in a mirror. Does it look the same on both sides of your nose? Have some fun creating a painting in half the time using **reflection** and **symmetry**!

## Materials:

white paper

full tissue box or stack of books

small mirror

washable paint

paintbrush

---

**reflect** bounce off an object
**symmetry** same on both sides of a centre line

## Steps:

1. Fold a piece of paper in half, open it back up and put it down on a table.

2. Ask an adult to help you place a mirror so it is standing up along the paper's fold. Use a tissue box or a stack of books to hold the mirror in place.

3. Looking through the mirror, paint one half of a symmetrical shape, such as half of a heart or half of a smiley face.

4. Before the paint dries, fold the paper back over itself, and carefully smooth your hand over where you painted.

5. Open the paper back up and allow it to dry. What does your shape look like?

# STAINED-GLASS MASTERPIECE

Light can create beautiful artwork. Stained glass is made up of **translucent**, coloured pieces of glass that form a pattern or design. Make your own art with light using some simple kitchen supplies!

## Materials:

clear, plastic window found on many pasta boxes and food packaging

PASTA

aluminium foil

scissors

stapler

washable marker pens

hole punch

black permanent marker

wool or string

## Beautiful shapes

Have you ever looked through a toy kaleidoscope? Do you know how it works? It uses light and reflection to repeat an image over and over again. Through a kaleidoscope, one small object can look like hundreds!

# Steps:

1. Use scissors to cut out the *transparent* window from a pasta box.

2. With a permanent marker pen, draw the outline of a fish on it. Add an eye and fish scales.

3. Colour in the picture with washable marker pens, making it colourful. Put it to one side.

4. Crumple a piece of aluminium foil into a ball. Then smooth it out.

5. Put the foil behind the clear image. Does the aluminium foil make your fish sparkle?

6. Create an ornament by stapling the foil behind the fish image. Cut around the image. Punch a hole in the top, and thread a piece of string through it. How is your artwork similar to stained glass?

**translucent** letting some light pass through
**transparent** easy to see through

# SEE THAT SOUND

Can you believe that certain sounds can actually break glass? You may wonder how this is possible. See for yourself with this simple project that allows you to make a bang!

## Materials:

small interlocking toy bricks

metal cake tin

tracing paper

small plastic cup or container

permanent marker

toy hammer or large wooden spoon

rubber band

## Tip:
If you can't get the interlocking pieces to move, replace them with something smaller, such as grains of rice.

## Steps:

1. Make a drum by placing a piece of tracing paper over the top of the plastic cup. Secure the paper with a rubber band.

2. Put the small interlocking toy bricks on top of the drum. Trace around the pieces with the marker pen.

3. Put the cake tin and the drum next to each other. Bang on the cake tin with the toy hammer.

4. Watch what happens to the interlocking pieces. Have they moved outside of your traced lines?

15

# MUSICAL RUBBER BANDS

Musical **instruments** make different sounds and have different **pitches**. That's why music is so much fun to listen to! Make your own instrument using rubber bands.

## Materials:

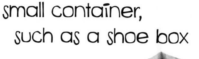

small container, such as a shoe box

rubber bands of different widths

### Tip:
If you don't have rubber bands of different widths, try pinching them at different points with one hand. At the same time, pluck with the other hand.

**instrument** something used to make music
**pitch** how high or low a sound is

## Steps:

1. **Place the rubber bands around the container.**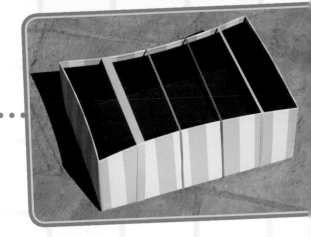

2. **Pull the rubber bands gently, and then let go. Which has a lower pitch — a thicker or thinner rubber band?**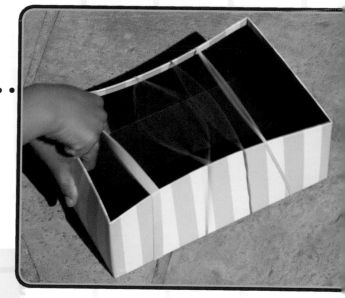

3. **Try making up a new song on your instrument.**

## Musical glasses!

Did you know that your drink can also be an instrument? Fill a couple of drinking glasses with different amounts of water. Gently tap near the top of each glass with the end of a pen or spoon. Which glass makes the lowest sound — the one with the most or least amount of water?

# BE A FOLEY ARTIST!

Turn on your favourite TV programme or film. Close your eyes and just listen. Can you tell from the sounds what is happening in the scene? People who create these sounds for TV programmes and films are called Foley artists. You can be a Foley artist using toys from your bedroom!

## Materials:

comic book or picture book

small toys made out of various materials, such as marbles or small interlocking toy bricks

plastic eggs or other small plastic containers

## Steps:

1. Pick a comic or story that has a lot of action. Try to find things in the story that you can match up with sounds, such as a loud boom, a door slamming or the rattle of a rattlesnake.

2. Use your toys to make noises to fit these scenes. Slide the toys across a hard surface or put them in plastic eggs and shake them. Try hitting them with your hand. Are you able to make sounds for each scene? Which sounds were the hardest to create? Which were the easiest?

3. Share your story and sounds with a friend or sibling.

# WHY IT WORKS

Would you like to know how these amazing experiments work? Here is the science behind the fun!

## PAGE 6 - FRIGHT NIGHT

Solid objects that cannot be seen through, such as a stuffed animal, block light. The shadow will show wherever there is a lack of light. Placing the torch close to the object will make a large shadow. Placing the torch further away from the object will make a smaller shadow. If the torch is held in different places, the shadow will become shorter or longer.

## PAGE 8 - SUN POWER

The toy blocked the Sun's **rays**, stopping the paper underneath it fading. Sun cream helps block the harmful ultraviolet rays from the Sun. This is why the paper covered in sun cream inside the CD case was protected.

## PAGE 10 - REFLECTION PAINTING

You drew only half of the shape because light hit the mirror, which reflected the same image as the image you had just drawn on the paper.

## PAGE 12 - STAINED-GLASS MASTERPIECE

The clear plastic is transparent, letting light through it. The permanent marker is **opaque**, and the washable marker pens are translucent. The aluminium foil bounces light in different directions, making the image sparkle.

## PAGE 14 - SEE THAT SOUND

When you hit the cake tin, it created **vibrations**. The vibrations from banging on the cake tin travelled through the air to the drum. When the surface of the drum vibrated, the interlocking toy bricks moved.

## PAGE 16 - MUSICAL RUBBER BANDS

The thicker the rubber band is, the slower it will vibrate, creating a lower-pitch sound. The thinner the rubber band is, the quicker it will vibrate, creating higher-pitch sounds.

## PAGE 18 - BE A FOLEY ARTIST!

Your toys make different sounds when you play with them, shake them or hit them against your hand. Some objects vibrate more when they hit one another, making sharper sounds. Others **absorb** the vibrations and make less noise or softer sounds.

**ray** line of light that beams out from something bright
**opaque** not letting light through
**vibration** fast movement back and forth
**absorb** soak up

# GLOSSARY

**absorb** soak up

**experiment** scientific test to find out how something works

**instrument** something used to make music

**opaque** not letting light through

**pitch** how high or low a sound is

**ray** line of light that beams out from something bright

**reflect** bounce off an object

**shadow** dark shape made when something blocks light

**symmetry** same on both sides of a centre line

**translucent** letting some light pass through

**transparent** easy to see through

**ultraviolet light** invisible form of light that can cause sunburn

**vibration** fast movement back and forth

# READ MORE

*Amazing Animal Communicators* (Animal Scientists), Leon Gray (Raintree, 2015)

*Pitch and Frequency* (Exploring Sound), Richard Spilsbury (Raintree, 2014)

*Reflecting Light* (Exploring Light), Louise Spilsbury (Raintree, 2015)

# WEBSITES

**www.bbc.co.uk/schools/scienceclips/ages/5_6/sound_hearing_whatnext.shtml**
Play some games to learn more about how sound and light work in the world around us.

**www.kidsdiscover.com/spotlight/sound-and-vibration/**
Discover fascinating facts about sound and vibration and take a look at some amazing photographs that help to illustrate the impact of sound.

# INDEX